the SLIGO Journal of Arts & Letters

Montgomery College
7600 Takoma Ave.
Takoma Park, MD 20912

Cover artwork:
"Rain" by Thuan-anh Nguyen

ISBN:

979-8-9863518-2-7

Fall 2023 / Spring 2024

The Staff

Michael LeBlanc, Editor-in-Chief
David Lott, Poetry Editor

Art Support:

Michael Anthony, Leeanna Earp, Norberto Gomez, Jenny Walton

Contributing Editors:

Joseph Couch, Ian Sydney March, Esther Schwartz-McKinzie,
Greg Wahl

Student Interns:

Adriana Regalado, Logo Design
Kyllie Castellanos & Julia Smith, Art Photography

Addendum to 2022-2023 issue: Joseph Couch should have been included in
the staff acknowledgments as Contributing Editor. Thanks for your work!

Acknowledgments

The Staff especially appreciates of the generous support received from Dr. Brad Stewart, Kim McGettigan, and Shelly Alves in the Takoma Park/ Silver Spring Provost's Office. Thank you to all the folks in the TPSS Art Department that help us collect, photograph, and display the beautiful artwork included in this issue. Thank you, also, to the faculty and staff at Montgomery College who help out the Journal in a myriad of ways.

Table of Contents

the SLIGO Journal

Poetry

How to Treat Root Rot
Mac McKinzie
First Place Winner, *Sligo Journal* Student Poetry Contest, 2023-2024

"i killed a plant once because i gave
it too much water. lord, i worry
that love is violence."
— José Olivarez, "Getting Ready to Say I Love You to My Dad, It Rains"

First, become your father.
Don his spaceman mosquito netting and
Ridiculous outside shoes.
Tromp out to the garden,
Notice that the yellowing you saw before
Just at the edges of the cane
Today hiked up its brittle skirts and
Plodded steady towards the center veins,
Bottom leaves already having
Bowed their heads in grief.

Become concerned.

Ask a woman with arms full of ferns
In the garden section of the home goods store,
"Do I need to repent? My cane's gone cattywampus."
She will mistake you for an employee;
You must shame-facedly admit
You only think you may have
Killed a plant.
A rift of indignance will form
At the ridge of her brow.

Buy good steel pruners and a bag of soil;
Back home, cover yourself in dirt
And wear your father's clothes. Become more like him,
Feel compelled to water things too much.
But with such devotion.

Push your hand
Deep into soil

And claw out the roots,
As though you are helping the cane give birth.
Hold it at arm's length and wash everything away.
Observe it painfully,
Comically naked and clearly close to death.

Sit heavy at the edge of the deck and turn it over.
Here's where your hands start to ache—
Rot dug its teeth into all but one or two
Of the precious live roots,
Ate heartily at the stalk. You take up your blades
And think Olivarez was right to worry.

It's only fair the cane stings at your hands.
Talk lovingly as you dissect its grotesque arteries.
After everything is cut away you both rest,
It stands weakly in fresh soil and you sit exhausted
On rain-soaked outdoor furniture. The skin of your palms
Has burst into searing flame,
And you have flung decay into the compost, satisfied.
Call up your dad and explain everything,
About the leaves and
How you loved
To see cool water
Running over them.
You will be readily forgiven.

After dinner, while you're sitting on the porch
The thing keels over, dead.

Self
Andrea Portillo

act
Salem Celentano
Second Place Winner, *Sligo Journal* Student Poetry Contest, 2023-2024

and my pain spills like ink,
staining everything it touches.
creating destruction,
destroying my hope.
yet my mind clears;
focused on one task.
the grip of my blade,
the sing of my flesh,
the blossoms planted.
a bittersweet garden forms,
spilling unto me like vines.
wrapping around my naked form.
once the task is done,
all that's left is the visage.
a smile
wiped tears
dried blood
hidden pain
and half-truths.
who am i to assume?
assume that i'm different?
assume that i'm special?
assume that i'm loved?
but you didn't hear this from me.
you only see my painted smile,
the dried, cracked remnants of my act.
and oh darling,
how i love to perform.

Breathe
Selam Legesse

Like rain caressing ocean floors, I feel
That I could strip the world of all its glory
In ways that words can sometimes fail to heal
The sick and ugly fragments of my story
A spider dancing in its lonely web
Creating little storms inside my mind
The land of dreams my only gentle ebb
If only I could leave this world behind
Instead of asking who I am I rest
Should doubt work long and hard to come and go
One day will come my very last goodbye
The last day that I'll ever want to know
Till then I ache and straighten out the mess
Of time, this matter, and a game of chess

Alleyway
Yujin Sasaki

Ursa Major
Terry Quill

Iphigenia
Barbara Callender

Don't give it my name
but my reasons were…
complex. I am the light gone
tired, the sorrow, the vigor
duty bears youth return.
What is freely given,
is never
a sacrifice.

He was nothing without
command, proud behind
a curtain of breastplate, gleaming
swords, the men, and gods – always
the gods – the happy sounds
of the camp, beloved
hatreds, cursed revenge.
I was already that
wind. Oh, my mother, she
cried a howling gale,
and it was almost enough;
but it takes much to fill
an old man's sail.

Like the tempest that drove
fate's sisters before me, some
say for love, but never her,
never her orders to carry me,
as it carried them. Yet
it could hardly have been
otherwise. I am manifest,
that roaring breath;
they are:
my destiny.
When I am a god
I will make requirements

of no one.

A doe? Don't be dull,
the moon has no hart. No
dear, it was my blood,
a woman's mess, my
offering. Like her, I chose
my knife, like her, I
held off the goddess,
like her, my secret
I went gladly.

AOS Burning Resolve—Deep-Rooted Malice

Charles Ross

Stars and Smiles
Madison Thomas

On When Two Black Poets Randomly Cross Paths in Our Nation's Capital
Derrick Weston Brown

For Reuben Jackson

You can't just pass a black poet on the roadside.
Sitting like a sage whole note;
a bench's back holding him like a scale.

You pull over. Stop. Hit your blinkers.
Because these moments, in these days & times
are urgent, prestissimo

& you can't tell this poet how overwhelmed
you are about everything: job security, inflation, weight gain
& diabetes lurking in your DNA, while also wrestling with love & loss.

& this has you wringing your hastened hands.
As you wait for him to finish
a tender worded phone call.

As you stroll into his hug
you want to tell him
that he is a sight for soft eyes

& salve for sore ears
as the world seems to have gone goose-step again
& doubling down is today's default

You both pull back & play black folk catch-up:
batting a birdie of questions between the two of you—
How you doing?

You good!?
How are your loved ones?
You been writing?

What you been writing?
Work?

Can't complain.

A piece of laughter here.
A shoulder slap.
A resting hand &

You can't stop smiling.
Even as a sob hums in your diaphragm
idling between grief & relief.
You speak in freedom suites
Drape the other in multi-hued
Comfort quilted arpeggios:

Take care
Keep on doing it
Good to see you

One more hug for the road
he requests & you oblige
sopping up this touch

as the both of you:
self-declared tender-hearted men
shelter-in-place   then turn away

Your own footsteps
are drum brush soft
to your car.

On the drive home
everything
is
gold & gold & gold & gold & gold & gold & gold & gold

Brothers Chillin' with Mr. Softee
Shirley Washington

Crane & Peach Water Vessel
Dana Idnay

Manufactured Eden
Blossom Anyanwu

There is magic in our palms, a portal to simulated suns
Trees stretch towards the pixelated heavens,
Emerald leaves shimmering with data-spun dewdrops
Our fingers reach out, brushing holographic bark
A phantom echo of the roughness, the smell, the lifeblood pulse of a real
forest
In this manufactured Eden, everything is perfect,
Airbrushed and hyperreal.
No thorns prick the rose,
No disasters mar the landscape.
We have a good thing here
Never mind the sleazy salesman,
Hiding in the corners of our oasis
Scroll past the panhandlers on our pixelated paths and their honeyed voices
Ignore the cracks and glitches in the screen
Go on, they implore us
For what are a few shadows,
A few whispers, a few cracks in the flawless veneer
Compared to the eternal peace this Eden offers?
No nightmares claw at your sleep here
No worries gnaw at your soul.
Only the soft pulse and steady hum of a dream handspun from pixels
So let us go on wandering, deeper into this oasis of unreal
Bathe in the synthesized sun,
Drown in the orchestrated birdsong
Inhale the fabricated breeze
Enjoy the faint taste of silicon on your tongue

What's in a Name?
Moss Do Carmo

I wonder what name
They will write on my grave.
What name will they use
In my eulogies?
I have gone by many,
But can never hold onto one.
They all seem to slide off me
Like an old silken robe.
I don't begrudge
My previous names.
Claudia is a prophecy,
One that connects me to Brasil.
Claude was an experiment,
One that helped me
Know myself better.
Moss was a happy accident,
A name that delighted me
For a couple of seasons.
They covered me well, at the time,
But soon became cold and ill fitting.
Will I ever find a name
That fits me like a glove?
Or will I be buried
Under a blank headstone?
One made of black granite
And engraved with roses
So I can forever be
A rose by any other name.

Crossroads
Dave Hysom

A Cultural Dance
Elielle Kayomb

Falling out of Love—A Reversal Poem
Brian Cortez-Flores

"Fuck Love"
as I shout
And glisten my eyes
The sun begins to shine
I'm running with relief
I'm reconnecting to me
I released everything
I'm single and I love it
I'm alone and I love it
This is what it feels like to let go
you can't have it anymore
And trail of love petals are gone
smile of butterflies
That exquisite spark
Is just a void
The love inside my heart
Cause love sucks
As I begin to fall out of love
I run out to the clean green fields
Who enjoy tantalizing my heart
And affection for men
As I stop giving satisfaction
Drifting up to the sky
As it travels to the winds
I say goodbye to my fellow balloon of heart
And heavy burden from my heart
Releasing a diluvial of emotions
An embrace
Never thought that it would end this way
Cleansing my soul for the new year
Beneath my head
Now there are droplets of rain
I'm falling apart
I'm not ready to release
I hate being single
I hate being alone

Sandstorm
Stella Biles

Soon I'll return to San Diego
Where rain won't ruin a beautiful day
My only wish is to wake up next to you
In the Cadillac Motel where we stayed
I can't bear to live in the treehouse we built
Along the evergreen coast
Back when you said you'd never quit
I didn't know it would hurt the most

Underneath a painted galaxy
Our toes curling in the sand
When our brown eyes met, electricity
So with that you took my hand
We carelessly danced on tabletops
Soaring through our interstate benders
Parading like bulls through a china shop
Ignoring stern looks from bartenders

Why do I want to lift you so high,
When all you do is bring me down?
Your eyes showed no limits, much like the sky
Back when we ran this tumbleweed town
Why do I want to pull you in,
When all you do is push me away?
You'd forgiven my every sin
Until we woke on that fateful day

Then the fog broke in
Leaving cracks in already broken windows
Palm trees swaying in the wind
With sand-stained cheeks, your negligence grows
Now in the desert I kneel
Dark clouds tumble beyond the horizon
My hands become cracked and peeled
Forgetting what it's like to hold you in them

The Hunted

Carter Cordle

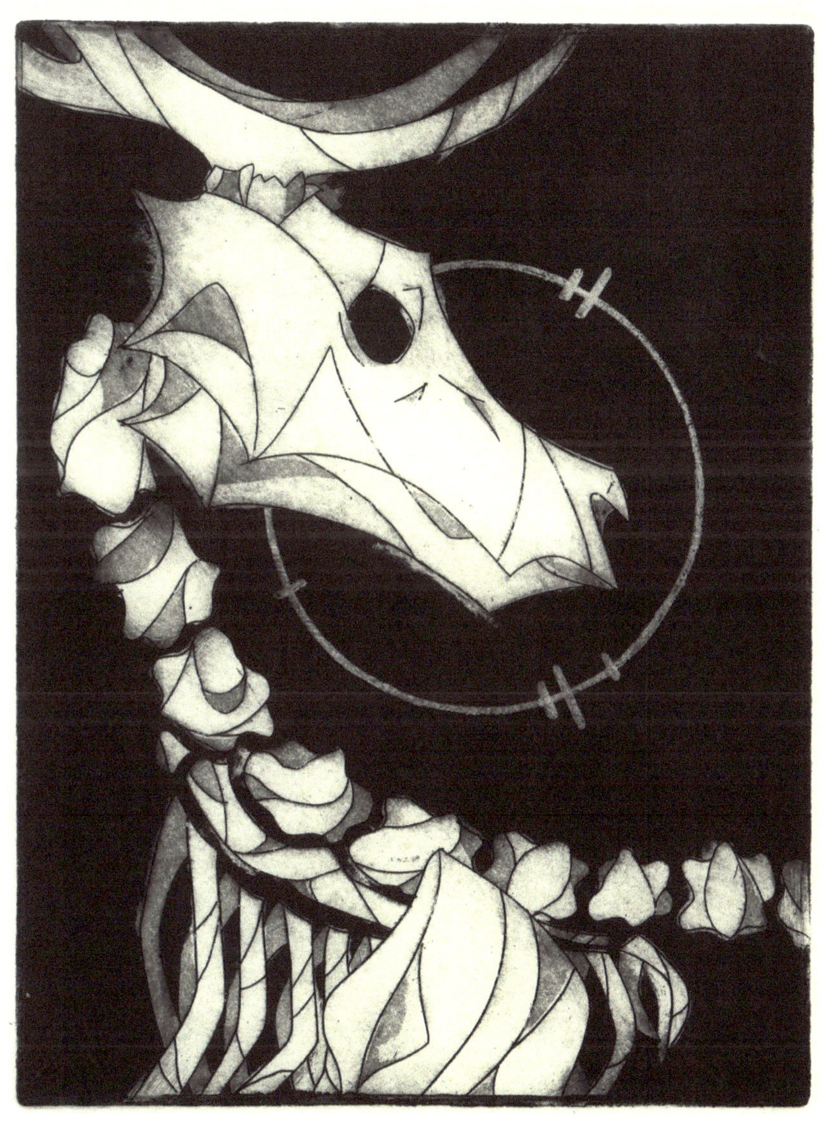

the SLIGO Journal

Fiction

Overlooked Reflection
Mariah Alvarez

Watchman
Sofia Hall-Levin

Wrangell, Alaska—1980

John Turner was a simple man. That's how everyone knew him—the man who lived a little ways out from the center of town, surrounded by land and lake, at an address everyone knew but never had occasion to visit. He had no wife or children, only his terrier, Willow, to keep him company. John would get into his red truck each morning and drive into town to sell his carvings. At midday, he'd eat a paper-wrapped sandwich for lunch. He'd take commissions for his carvings—a few animal figures to be sold at the hunting equipment store or a big spoon to wrap in ribbon and gift to a relative at their wedding. John would also sell whatever he liked—re-creations of things he'd seen on his tours or busts he'd been working on for years and lost interest in—faces half unfinished and mouths open wide. John would bend down to offer a piece of strawberry candy to the children who entered his shop and reaffirm their parents' claims that spinach was in fact how Popeye—and John— got so big and strong. John would close up shop at six and patronize Macie's Diner. He ordered the same meal every night, meatloaf with mashed potatoes and green beans, before climbing back into his truck and heading out past the tree line. John was a Vietnam vet with a purple heart and a deeply quiet, private man. Everyone in Wrangell, Alaska knew these things about John Turner and not much else.

Only John knew what happened once he drove down that long road in his truck. Macie often wondered, after he'd paid his bill and left a tip, if he liked to carve his pieces in front of a fireplace, filled with glowing yellow and orange flames, or in a chair on the dock looking out at the water and rim of woods as daylight faded. Who had John been before he blew into Wrangell and decided to stay?

John himself wasn't sure, this was his life now, and he had the right to keep to himself. He knew everything there was to know about the other townspeople. That's how he made his living, of course, creating pieces for their special occasions. The townspeople kept nothing to themselves, they weren't secret, and they loved having guests over. John wasn't like that. That's why he was so surprised to receive a knock on his door at seven in the morning. He didn't bother to pull on a pair of pants over his boxers. Anyone bothering him this early deserved to get an eyeful. He dragged his feet along the teakwood floor, narrowly missing tripping over fast-asleep Willow, and threw open the door, not bothering to check the eyehole first. On his front porch stood a Latin girl, maybe 16 or 17, curly brown hair and a duffel bag slung over her shoulder.

John wrapped his thin robe around himself and crossed his arms on his chest. "I don't want any Girl Scout cookies." He went to close the door, but the girl jammed her foot inside.

"John Turner?"

"Who's asking?"

"My name's Carmen and I'm your daughter."

John laughed. "That's funny." He managed to close the door. Damn town kids and their jokes. He went to brew himself a cup of coffee, ignoring the knocking and yelling on the other side of the door. Willow slept through it all, he never claimed to be a guard dog.

The knocking died down as John prepared his sandwich and set out Willow's kibble. He got dressed for the day in his self-imposed uniform. He opened the front door once again and saw the girl—Carmen—sitting on the stairs. "What're you still doing here?"

"I don't have anywhere else to go." She looked up over her shoulder at John.

"Come on in." John didn't buy her story, but he wasn't about to let the kid sit outside all day. "You hungry?" he asked once they were both inside.

"Starving."

Carmen dropped her bag by the front door and walked around the cabin, snooping in all his stuff, flipping through his photo albums as John whipped up some eggs and bacon. Willow circled Carmen and sniffed her, before rolling over with his belly up. "Hi, puppy!" Carmen exclaimed, crouching down to pet him.

She sat down at the table just as John came over with two plates, one of which he laid down in front of her. The teenager dug into the food quickly, keeping her eyes downcast, as she swallowed, barely chewing. John drew patterns into the drying egg yolk on his plate as the, frankly disturbing, noises slowed. "You've got the wrong guy."

"You're John Turner, are you not?"

"Well, yeah, but there's gotta be tons of John Turners 'round."

Lonesome
Shirley Washington

Chaos Unfolding
Kyllie Castellanos

Carmen crossed her arms and leaned back in her chair. "Two others within a hundred-mile radius. I checked the white pages."

"Well, maybe one of them's your dad," John said and nodded, that must be it.

"Checked in with them too, one's too young, the other's too old. Plus, I found an article about Vietnam vets with your name and this town in the newspaper. Mom said you were a soldier. Must've been fate, then." Either this girl was crazy or stupid.

"No such thing as fate, only coincidence."

"S'pose so, or maybe it's a miracle." And if only those were real, John wouldn't be getting punished like this right now.

"Well, sorry to break it to you, kid, but the miracle machine ain't workin' today. I'm not your dad." Carmen wiped her mouth with the back of her hand. She wasn't even listening to him, was she? "So, then, is there someone I can call to come get you?" he asked. The house didn't have a line, but there was a booth in town.

"No. I'm staying right here." Alright, that's how it was gonna be. John got up from his seat and gathered the plates to wash.

John hadn't taken a day off work in—actually—he couldn't quite remember the last time he neglected to open the shop. But what was he supposed to do? Leave this stranger in his home or take her with him?

He took down the few board games he'd managed to buy over the years. He'd never had company over since he took the place on, but Willow wasn't the worst Connect Four opponent, that pot was his at the end of every night. Carmen, however, beat him every time, taking her wins as a chance to grill him on all sorts of personal details.

"What do you do for work?" she asked, sipping from her mug of his coffee.

"Well, most've my income is from the pension but it's not enough to live on, so I also own a shop." John got to start this round, placing his puck in the center column.

"And?" Carmen made her move, placing her puck next to his.

"And I sell wood-stuffs, a few signs here and there from other shops around, mostly small stuff—your turn by the way—but, uh, I did a set of custom tables a few years back."

"They should call you John Carpenter then. Wait! No, I've got one, John Wood-Turner!" With that last move, she won again, having successfully distracted him. He was a soldier for Christ-sake, no way he's lost strategy this fast!

Carmen laughed at his dumbfounded face. "You're nothing like how I imagined you'd be."

"How's that?" John lifted an eyebrow.

"Well, for one, you're terrible at games. I always thought my dad would be the best player."

John's face turned to a scowl. "Screw you, I'm great at games… and I'm not your dad!" Carmen just giggled and took out the little tray on the bottom of the game, causing all the pucks to scatter on the floor.

The questions just kept coming. When did you fight in the war? Where are you from? When'd you move here? Before John knew it, the sun was setting, and he hadn't gotten any information from Carmen about when she'd be leaving. He took the couch for the night, so she'd get the bed in the only room with a lock. His back would hate him in the morning. Willow committed the ultimate betrayal, leaving him on his makeshift bed to sleep with Carmen.

*****

Ellis and John sat side to side, backs against the trunk of a tree. Night slowly fell as the two friends spoke, trading stories back and forth. "Man, I'm so ready to get out of here," John said. "I'd give anything to eat a meal cooked by my mom again. Man, she could fix up just about anything! Your mom cook much?" John didn't wait for a reply. "I know exactly what I'mma do when I get out of here," He carried on, sleepiness slurring his words, "I'mma buy a ring and propose to my girl." He took a picture of a dark-haired, olive-skinned woman out of his pocket, forcing Ellis to squint in the waning light.

"She's gorgeous."

John hummed. "Isadora, how I adore ya." Ellis laughed at the rhyme and swallowed against the thing in his throat, he thought there'd never been such a beautiful name for a woman. Truth is, there was no girl waiting for Ellis to come home. There was no home to come back to. Hell, he'd either fail to make it out of this place or escape to some other end of the globe.

See, Ellis enlisted because it was his chance to get away. As a child, every decision was made by his mother and father. He couldn't do anything to make them proud, to make them see him. Nothing smoothed the tight clench of Mom's mouth or the stern furrow of Dad's brow. Not when he almost became valedictorian (get it next time), or received his first paycheck (waste of time), not even when he brought his first girlfriend home (could do better). The first time his father told him he was proud to have him as a son was when he broke the news about his enlistment. That feeling of validation zipped through him and he knew that he could never come back 'cause he'd never stop seeking that feeling. No one saw him off, he left on his own as soon as he could and didn't look back. And here he was, the only thing left of the old him was his name and a few papers.

But John… John had everything, a family that was proud of him, a girl that loved him. Everything Ellis was missing. It was a stupid mistake that Ellis made, letting John fall asleep, falling asleep himself after he'd promised to keep watch. And then it was all red and sound so loud it hurt your ears and pain so sharp in his leg that—

A hand touched his shoulder and John shot up from the couch, swinging an arm out to defend himself. Carmen stepped back just in time to dodge his fist, Willow whining beside her. The two of them took a moment to catch their breath before she spoke up. "I think he needs to be let out." John got up, with no great difficulty, and started his day with the same old ache in his leg.

✳✳✳✳✳

John brought Carmen into town with him, he felt uneasy about leaving her at home alone but he had to open up the shop and make an appearance in town. Wrangell was first and foremost a tourist destination for the Tlingit fishing culture, something he came to learn only after moving there. A few days closed meant the loss of a good portion of sales. Upon entering the store, Carmen's eyes skipped over the rows and rows of miniature animal carvings on the shelves, a favorite of tourists who wanted a keepsake before taking the ferry back to the mainland. She picked up a tin of wax finish from the supplies section and held it to her nose before nodding, placing it back down, and coming to stand next to him behind the counter. John worried about what she thought of the store and missed two familiar faces sneaking in before he could flip the sign around. Maybe he'd commission a shopkeeper's bell from the metalsmithing store across the way.

"John! We didn't see you yesterday. Didn't set up shop?" Clemence asked. He and Gladys, the old couple who ran the antique store next to John's, were always in his business, literally.

John elbowed Carmen beside him. "My—uh—niece came to town so we had to spend some time together before she leaves." Carmen waved at the older pair. "Soon." He could feel her stiffen.

"Oh, how sweet," Gladys cooed, holding onto Clemence's arm. "We didn't know you had siblings!" John smiled tightly. "Oh, well, we'll let you get set up. Just wanted to make sure everything was right with old John."

"As rain, ma'am, right as rain." The couple chuckled as they left the storefront.

"Your niece?" Carmen walked in front of the counter.

"What should I have said? My maybe-daughter who hitchhiked her way to my cabin?" That didn't warrant a snarky reply. The tense silence was saved by the door opening, signaling the first customer of the day.

Carmen wasn't such a bad coworker. Everyone wanted to come into John's store and spend their money on wood oil or a small badger figurine just to get a look at his adorable niece: *John, how come you never talk about your family?* So a good day's cash was made before closing time came around. Carmen swept the floor as John flipped the sign from open to closed. 5 pm. An early dinner couldn't hurt.

"Good job, kid."

Carmen stopped sweeping and turned around to face John. "What now, back to the cabin?"

"Nah, we're getting dinner at Macie's. Best in town."

Macie practically threw herself over Carmen, thanking her for forcing our John to take a day off, I swear I never get a break from his ugly mug. She brought out a slice of pie, on the house, that John wasn't allowed to touch by her instruction. He left a tip under the receipt that paid for it twice over, just to see her smile through the window as he and Carmen left.

And so started their routine for a few days, Carmen would come with him to work and they'd eat dinner together, either at home or at Macie's. It was nice. Domestic. One day, she went snooping and found the gun in the kitchen cabinets so he had to tell her to stop looking

Star Within—But Not Confined

Raynier Hernandez

The World Around
Jade Rivas

through his shit. They laughed together in a way John hadn't laughed in years. Then he came back from walking Willow one morning. He couldn't find Carmen but her shoes were still by the door. John unleashed Willow and walked into his bedroom to find her sitting on the bed, hunched over a shoebox, holding his purple heart with his real name—Ellis Miller—engraved on the back.

"I'm not who you think I am." Carmen jumped and looked over her shoulder as John spoke.

"I know." She left the room and came back with a picture of John, the real John, with his sweetheart Isadora. "You don't look like him at all, but I came all the way here 'cause I don't know why I'm so different from my mom and I thought I'd figure it out in him. But I was just tricking myself, thinking I'd finally found him. And I didn't want to go home, I wasn't ready." John nodded, he got it. "So, Ellis, huh? That you?"

"I haven't been Ellis in a long time, I think I'm just John."

"John fits you better." She shrugged.

"You think so?"

Carmen hummed and nodded her head, bending down to paw at Willow, who'd been whining from the lack of attention.

She straightened up and stopped her petting, much to Willow's dismay. "John? I'm ready to go home now."

She asked if he could drive her into town to call home and teased him about not having a line in the cabin. They got in the truck, Willow squeezing in the thin parts of the bench left between John and Carmen as they made the short drive. John stood outside to give her some privacy, only turning around to provide her with more quarters each time she asked. He graciously ignored the tears on her face contrasting with her smile, but provided the hug she asked for, tucking her head under his chin and swaying them back and forth. She shoved him away with a laugh. "Don't get too soft on me now, old man."

"You know, you're like me after all." If John didn't know what he did, Carmen could very well have been his daughter. The thought made his chest tight. "Maybe a little bit too much in fact, 'cept for the ugly, of course." He ran away with a laugh as she tried to chase him.

"Up yours, Grandpa!"

He bought two tickets to the ferry the next morning and brought enough cash for the both of them to get a taxi to a midway point where Carmen and Isadora could reunite without anyone having to go too far. On the way to their destination, they barely scratched the surface of that painful story. John owed it to Carmen to tell her of her father's death and about the kind of man he was. John was not ready to tell her everything, and there was nowhere near enough time, but what he could say filled the space in the journey between his home and Carmen's reunion with her mom. And the embrace they shared, Carmen's face in her mother's hands, the love only a mother can have for her child, it was all too intimate for John to see something he'd never had. Carmen and Isadora got on the bus together and John watched it leave. As Carmen waved goodbye, he waved back, feeling raw as an exposed wire.

He wasn't ready to go back to Wrangell quite yet, choosing instead to walk around the town he was in. Maybe it had taken Carmen for John to realize he never really did leave behind that kid he had been. He had been frozen in time as the rest of him grew older, never wanting to give anything of himself up. So he'd hopped on the ferry to the first town that had heard no mention of an Ellis Miller or a John Turner. He got himself a routine he never strayed from, walking Willow, eventually opening up the shop, and eating dinner at the diner instead of cold MREs. But Carmen made him stray from that safe routine he'd set for himself.

There was so much that he still wanted to ask her—her and Isadora. How did they not know of John's death? Did John and Isadora know each other as well as he'd let on? And the questions they'd ask him back... if they ever met again. He found himself thinking about John, the real John, and Isadora's sweetheart and father to Carmen, the man whose name he carried with him out of what... guilt for causing his death, respect for the man he called friend, fear of knowing himself after the war? What about the sides to John that none of them ever saw? He found himself thinking of poor Isadora's worry for her runaway daughter and wondering if his own mother could ever feel that way... and what about the real John's mother, who lost her son in the war and knew nothing of her granddaughter? He found himself thinking about the years spent in solitude, locked away from Wrangell. He found that now his life seemed a little bit lonelier without someone to beat him at Connect Four. And the realization up, he saw a phone number and a message at the bottom. *Visit anytime.*

Man's Best Friend
Carter Cordle

The Fracturing
Eden Roy

Triptych
Eden Roy

At the intersection of two ancient, cobbled alleyways was a solitary art studio, its humble exterior of roughly stuccoed stone masking the otherworldly realm within.

Here, time is paused; nothing exists if not smeared oil. As though suspended in a realm of eternal chiaroscuro, paintings burned lay abandoned against the walls. This chamber was nearly a canvas in and of itself, adorned with sketches, indiscernible notes, and the remains of artistic endeavors long forgotten. The boundaries of art and reality were smudged beyond distinction. The mirrors and windows were covered in cloth and curtains for his protection, the only glimpses outside this realm confined to canvas.

The light from cheap candles let out only wispy echoes against the darkness of night – not-good-enough-not-good-enough-not-good-enough. How could an artist understand and capture beauty if he cannot see beyond the shadows?

Frustrated and determined, Giovanni tugged the handle of the weathered dresser to his right, pulling out a fresh candle and lighting its wick. He drew it close to the image before him and narrowed his eyes in scrutiny. Not-good-enough.

In a fleeting moment of inspiration, he scribbled a mathematical diagram on spare parchment and held it against the painting, searching for a sense of perspective within this failure. He was only met with a crushing sense of inadequacy. With an exasperated sigh, he tossed it aside, the parchment joining the numerous scribbles haphazardly strewn in a rune around him on the floor.

He stared momentarily at his palette – a chaotic mosaic of pigments, each hue a testament to his relentless pursuit of perfection – before gathering his resolve and starting again. Correcting-correcting-correcting. If the world were to deny him beauty, then he had no choice but to create his own.

In this studio, he was no longer an ugly spectacle to jeer and giggle at, but this does not mean he was safe; the eyes of his subjects loomed and judged and scrutinized. Hundreds of paintings and oils, pigments blended into biblical figures. They watched him paint; not-good-enough-not-good-enough-not-good-enough. His skin grew thick at the fingertips, and his back calcified from his hunch over his paintings. The eyes, through the years, they-watched-they-watched-they-watched. It was never-ending, this pursuit, but he was determined. But how could he capture beauty if he had never known it?

This was the only way he knew how – to-try-to-try-to-try. Until, greeted by the waxing light of dawn diffusing through the crevices between the curtains, he laid his final brushstroke and met her. She was perfection, a beauty, a Venus.

The freshly dried oil slicked into shadows that stretched over her face. Venetian Red seamlessly glimmered into a soft blush, and the pigment that stained Giovanni's hands cascaded down the beautiful figure's shoulders. Blooming to life and escaping from her canvas, the newborn Venus was met only by a face of pure horror from the artist who created her.

It was silent for a moment as Giovanni struggled to remember to breathe.

Then, panic.

Then, a blundering scramble to the door.

Then, at the door handle, his flee slowly stops. Bewitched with curiosity, he found himself unable to turn away from a heretic's life. His eyes met hers; their faces a juxtaposition. One, a goddess's flawless, porcelain skin, and the second, a face marred with the unforgiving stamp of disfigurement. She was the ideal, perfection, everything he had ever wanted to be. Venus' splendor and energy seemed to glow in the bath of dawn's light, and her lips curved into a kind smile. Giovanni's voice was caught in his throat before he bowed his head before her. "Venus," he stammered, "Please help me; I am cursed with a face that repels the world."

Her voice, a sweet melody, settled in his ears like the wind.

She offered him two choices: beauty or love.

Pausing, he found himself uncertain of what could save him from his wretched existence. He gazed down at the distorted, mottled skin on his hand. He had only ever known the life of an outcast, as if he were a grotesque animal confined to the shadows of this world. In the end, solitude was the only peace he could find.

He was always filled with envy at the sight of those who had found love. It was never something he had thought could be within his reach.

He thought, surely, that if he were freed of his cursed appearance, those around him would see him and love him. Then, he could have both! He ached for beauty, to even hold a flame to the perfection of Florentine architecture or the pieces of the great masters. With a deep breath and an excited smile, he declared:

"Beauty."

A shimmering radiance began to envelop his skin, his features metamorphosizing from deformity to symmetrical, flawless perfection. Overwhelmed with anticipation, he scrambled to his desk and searched desperately for a mirror or glass, but there was nothing-nothing-nothing. Like a madman set aflame, he ran to his windows, pulling aside the curtains that protected him from the world.

In the reflection of the windowpane, he saw the face of a man who had never known scorn or dismay. The warmth of the rising sun framed his image like an exquisite masterpiece he could never have dreamed of painting. Tears began to well up in his eyes, falling and caressing his smoothed skin.

He turned to face his savior, but she was gone.

*****

Reborn, he stepped foot outside, the streets washed with the early morning light. The air seemed to quiver with anticipation.

As he strolled into the bustling market down the street from him, a hushed silence fell over the crowd. Pausing their gossip and merriment, his neighbors' eyes watched Giovanni's every move. The women excitedly whispered to each other, the gesturing of their fingers fluttering like birds taking flight.

The voices grew louder and louder.

The air, taut with admiration, began to fray like splintering twine into unease. He heard the whisperings, the speculations: He was a god, a result of a Faustian pact, a prince from a faraway land. He couldn't escape them, the eyes-the-eyes-the-eyes; they were everywhere-everywhere-everywhere. They were watching everything, every move and every twitch of the muscle; they watched and conjectured and jeered.

The images of the past echoed within his mind – the chasing,

Late Night Lofi
Tanisha McIver

the sharpness of their cruelty, the blood spilled. The forms in which his bruised body contorted in agony on this road. His crooked hand reaching for help, only to grasp rejection. No matter if he was ugly or beautiful, he was never anything more than a spectacle in their eyes. Whether through envy or scorn – they would never love him.

It was as if a rift still separated him from the world – on one side, he stood alone; on the other, they stared. The eyes, oh God, they-stared-they-stared-they-stared.

He would never escape the stares. He just wanted to be left alone. The faces of the crowd smeared into those from his past – they were judging him the same! They could never understand! They were going to hurt-and-hunt-and-harm-and-

He scrambled together his purchase and tossed a few coins the shopkeeper's way, hurriedly gathering himself and rushing towards his home. It was safe there, so-safe-so-safe-so-safe.

He slammed the door behind him and triple-checked the locks. One-two-three-one-two-three. He ran to the curtains and tied them closed. He stood there, dizzyingly panting and staring at his creation, the paint still fresh and wet.

Amidst the brushstrokes of the sea and pearls and shells, the figure where Venus once lay was awash with white plaster, as though she had never existed.

*****

The attention was wounding and never-ending; they would only sneer and speculate-speculate-speculate. He found himself once more cornered away from the world, like a freak in a cage. He desperately covered the mirrors and windows once more, cowering in fear from his image. He cried to the heavens, to the blank white smears on his masterpiece,

"Venus, please, I was a fool. Please, grant me love. I didn't understand, please."

He lunged for his paintbrush, deciding to try once more. However, it slipped-slipped-slipped right through his softened skin. As if it were grains of sand, his paintbrush, his desires, his savior, tricked its way out of his fingertips every time he tried. After all, his calluses, once the scaffolding to his artistic abilities, had dissipated like wind.

Thus, he maddeningly labored before his canvas like a servant kneeling before his king; he tried-and-tried-and-tried. He tried to mimic her features and bring her to life once more.

His back hunched with the time spent toiling over this canvas; the drawn curtains denied him the sun until his skin grew pale and veiny. Calluses overtaking his skin once more, he gripped the paintbrush as though his life depended on it. His perfect features decayed with exhaustion, his great chiseled cheekbones riddled with eyebags, his skin mottled with frustrated wrinkles.

No matter how hard he labored, it was not-good-enough-not-good-enough-not-good-enough. He rotted before this easel, surrounded by his protective sigils of maddened scribbles and canvases cast aside.

Oh, how he-prayed-he-prayed-he-prayed. He begged and pleaded with Venus to return once more. But she clearly snubbed him, she denied her loyal subject, so he picked up this canvas and threw it against the wall.

He hit a mirror, hidden behind a cloth, sending glass fragments splaying across his messy floor. He shot up from his stool, running to the canvas, apologizing to her. A shard of mirror glazed the sole of his foot.

He stopped in his tracks and picked up his foot to assess the wound. Crimson blood dripped down its side, framing his reflection: The remnants of a handsome face fallen to ruin. Wrinkles and calluses painted his skin like great valleys and mountains. Sneaking through the window, the whispers of dawn, of a new day, danced on the edges of his jaw and nose.

He studied his new face, smoothing his fossilized fingers over the ridges and foreign features. The testaments to his artistry, to his craft, to his dedication. His fingers, they were perfect once more!

The reflection of Venus happily gazed upon himself. His face crept into a smile before he lost himself in a fit of laughter and gratefully kissed the fractured glass.

Dennis
Doris Eisen

Monkey Performing Stand-up
Alicia Valderrama

Contributors

Mariah Alvarez is a young woman who first found her love for the art world with simple cartoon doodles and paintings with her grandfather on the daily newspaper. As she got older, she used the old school disposable cameras during family vacations and birthdays, which sparked her interest in photography at a young age. Since then, Mariah has viewed all artistic media as a new challenge to accomplish and explore.

Blossom Anyanwu is a second-year student at Montgomery College and is currently pursuing an Associate's Degree in General Studies STEM with a Data Science concentration. Academically she enjoys learning about statistics and anthropology, and in her free time, she enjoys writing.

Roy Beri is an art student at Montgomery College.

Stella Biles is currently getting ready to graduate from MC in May before attending nursing school at the Universities at Shady Grove this fall. When she's not studying the art of biology, however, she's immersing herself in the art of language. In elementary school, she found creative writing to be a great way to escape reality, and has since then written many songs, short stories, and poems. The creative writing process allows her to organize the jumble of words in her brain and turn them into something tangible. She finds joy in taking aspects of her imagination and rearranging them into rhymes and prose. She is now looking forward to sharing a portion of her anthology with *The Sligo Journal*.

Derrick Weston Brown holds an MFA in Creative Writing from American University. He is a native of Charlotte, North Carolina, and resides in Mount Rainier, Maryland. He was an adjunct professor of English and Literature at Prince George's Community College and is full-time Creative Writing faculty at the Duke Ellington School of the Arts, Cinematic Arts & Media Production Department (CAMP).

Barbara Callender is an adult student at Montgomery College. She plans to attend the University of Maryland in 2024 as an English major with a concentration in creative writing and poetry.

Kyllie Castellanos, a Washington D.C. native, discovered her love for art early on, attending an art-focused grade school and learning from three influential mentors in high school. Inspired by artists John Singer Sargent, Alphonse Mucha, James Jean, and Loish, she now channels her passion into illustration. Kyllie's diverse work explores various narratives across mediums like oil paint, charcoal, and pastel, captivating her audience with story and vibrant colors.

For Salem Celentano, poetry has always been a safe space, giving them an outlet to express their emotions in a healthy way. They hope you enjoy their writing and the works of others in this journal.

Carter Cordle is an artist from Gaithersburg, MD. He uses art as a projection of his interests and feelings, hoping to create a space where others feel encouraged to do the same.

Brian Cortez-Flores is a prolific writer who is passionate with a heart for storytelling that is a self-reflection of every version of his life. He is an adventurous soul who explores the lens of his next chapter while completing a manuscript of 100 poems.

Moss Do Carmo (any pronouns) is a queer Brazilian-American writer. When they're not writing, they can be found reading, listening to podcasts, or playing Minecraft.

Doris Eisen graduated as an art major from Queens College in New York City. She has taught art to both children and adults. She has been an active printmaker (mostly etching and lithographs) for over 30 years. During that time, she has exhibited in many shows and won many prizes. The collected works of Doris Ellen Eisen is available on Amazon.

Sofia Hall-Levin is a Silver Spring native and has been fiction writing since a young age. Sofia looks forward to attending the University of Maryland in the Fall of 2024.

Monster Burger
Andrea Portillo

Roi (King)
Roy Beri

Raynier Hernandez is an art student at Montgomery College.

Dave Hysom is an emerging visual artist who works in charcoal, oil, and acrylic paints. He is a Montgomery County native and is currently living his dream, making art and raising his three children with his wife in Silver Spring.

Dana Idnay is an 18-year-old college student from Rockville, Maryland. She has enjoyed painting and drawing from a very early age, and has always loved performance art. She recently became interested in ceramic clay mediums, after taking a ceramics class as a dual enrollment high school student. The piece, "Crane and Peach Vessel" was her first big project using stoneware.

Elielle Kayomb was born in Congo (DRC). She received her Associate's Degree in Fine Arts at Montgomery College in 2023. Elielle has exhibited at The Museum of Science and Technology in Chicago, The Sarah Silberman Art Gallery, and the King Street Gallery in Maryland. Her Painting "The Bearer" won First Place in the Montgomery Art Association Juried Exhibit Student Show in 2022. Her painting "Ophelia's Pain" is currently in the Montgomery County Council Show. She is now studying for her Bachelor's Degree of Fine Arts and Master's Degree of Arts in Teaching at the Maryland Institute College of Art.

Selam Legesse is a second-year general studies major at Montgomery College.

Tanisha McIver is an art student at Montgomery College.

Mac McKinzie is an apologetic plant-killer and poet whose work has been previously published in the *Arlington Literary Journal* and the *Plum Creek Review*. She hopes that readers regard her contribution as a PSA against overwatering.

Thuan-anh Nguyen took this photo on a rainy day at home. Inspiration can come from the most unexpected places: a rainbow, a raindrop, or the alley underneath your apartment window.

Andrea Portillo is a Salvadoran artist exploring her identity through art.

Terry Quill is a retired toxicologist and D.C. attorney who has always had an interest in the arts. Having a little time now to spend on new pursuits, he is enjoying visual arts with the help of Montgomery College. Terry takes advantage of a number of the College's introductory art classes, including printing, drawing, and painting.

Jade Rivas, a visual artist with seven years of creative exploration, holds an Associate's Degree in Art, specializing in Graphic Design. Focused on painting, her work delves into themes of feminism, social injustices, and the transformative influence of music, reflecting a deep connection to mindfulness. In her featured artwork, an intriguing experimentation of chaos versus order takes center stage. The goal was to explore texture, creating controlled chaos that reflects Jade's unique personality in this self-portrait. Each deliberate brushstroke contributes to the narrative, inviting viewers to contemplate the interplay of elements. This artwork encapsulates Jade Rivas's commitment to pushing artistic boundaries, showcasing a fusion of passion and skill within the broader tapestry of the art world.

Charles Ross really started taking art seriously during his high school years. During his car rides to and from school, his headphones blaring with music, those were his most creative moments. He would spend days, weeks even, translating all the stories and feelings of the characters he had made onto paper. He was like a sponge, inspired by the media he consumed, but turning them into his own feelings, passions, and stories.

Eden Roy is a student with a focus on museum studies, ancient art history, and anthropology. Her creations are inspired by Impressionism and explorations of timeless human experiences; ultimately, her goal is to curate exhibits that both evoke emotions and are accessible to all.

Yugin Sasaki is an art student at Montgomery College.

Madison Thomas is a mostly 2D mixed media artist aspiring to become a graphic designer, who also enjoys stickers, as seen in her work "Stars and Smiles." Her inspirations are anime, nature, and her artist grand-mother, Golshah Agdasi. She is running on a rushing river of emotional creativity, towards the goal of self-actualization. She hopes to someday succeed alongside the other achieving stars of our world. But before she becomes a star, she must gain and maintain her smile.

Alicia Valderrama takes studio and digital art classes. She also took one ceramics class during Spring 2023.

Shirley Washington is a lifelong learner who is a six-time graduate of Montgomery College (with honors). Her photographic trilogy, "Jour-neying Home," is available via Amazon.